8 STEPS FROM FREEDOM

8 Steps From Freedom

BREAKING FREE FROM THE FEAR OF JUDGMENT

Lady Carolyn Byrd

BYRD FAMILY BOOKS

Byrd Family Books

Contents

Introduction

The pervasive fear of judgment infiltrates numerous facets of a person's life, extending from your relationships to your overall well-being. This insidious fear seizes control over self-perception, self-care, and self-love. Within the fathomless reservoir of your being, beneath layers of external opinions, lies an inner you trapped within a paralyzing emotional state. One is petrified to advocate for themself and incapable of embracing your inner confidence. You have thus far excelled in concealing your true self behind a counterfeit mask, safeguarding your fragile facade. Yet, beneath this veil lies a soul paralyzed by the dread of judgment and haunted by the question, "*Am I enough?*"

Acknowledging and addressing this fear is vital as it can impede you from taking risks, exploring new experiences, or pursuing aspirations. Succumbing to this fear perpetuates an unending cycle of rationalizing complacency in your life.

To ascend beyond the fear of judgment requires cultivating self-assurance, contesting pessimistic self-talk, and establishing coping mechanisms for handling criticism and rejection. By confronting this trepidation, you can attain the confidence and resilience necessary to pursue personal goals and cultivate a fulfilling existence. It is time to emancipate yourself from the unseen shackles that have weighed heavily upon your spirit and entwined around your mind – obscuring the illuminating truth of your inherent worth. The moment has arrived to reclaim yourself!

My Story

As long as I can recall, the assertion, "Sticks and stones may break my bones, but words can never harm me," echoed throughout my childhood. We frequently recited a refrain when the schoolyard bully would assail us verbally, mocking our usual adolescent awkwardness, such as our knocked knees, crooked or missing teeth, hand-me-down clothing, or our head whose bodies had not yet fully matured. In my case, all of the above, plus being born with a white scalp in the back of my head, produced bright white hair. My keen nose was the subject of ridicule and constant laughter from my siblings. I was the butt of all the old lady witch jokes, with endless hair pulling as I traversed the school halls or stairs, perpetual stares, and pointing. Then one day, my body and head aligned, and I grew into a nicely developing young lady. At 13 years old, I looked in the mirror and thought, "I'm not so bad now." However, that thought was short-lived, and my worldview was about to change dramatically.

It was a sunny summer afternoon, and I had volunteered at the veterans' hospital for a few weeks. I exited the bus and began strolling down the street, always enraptured by nature's beauty, specifically the sky, and water. Walking across the street from my home, I gazed up at the sky and silently prayed, as I did every day. Suddenly, a voice shouted at me, "Look at you, walking around here with your nose in the air, thinking you are cute!" I spun toward the familiar voice, and my heart sank. "No, I'm not," I retorted, "and I don't think I'm cute!" But the voice snickered, "Yes, you were; you think you're so cute!" Broken-hearted, I went inside, my eyes stinging with tears. It crushed my spirit, and I vowed never to look up again while walking because I never wanted to feel that type of judgment again. Criticism, judgment, and misunderstanding plagued me, and the worst part was the opinion was so far from the truth. I couldn't explain myself because I felt judged. From that day on, whenever I entered a room or was in a group, I did it with my head down, fearing judgment. Around that same time, I began hearing the phrase "the darker the berry, the sweeter the juice" from the man my mother married. He constantly implied that I was not dark enough and that darker-skinned people were sweeter, comparing me to my sister, who had a beautiful chocolate complexion. Always implying I was not good enough, he would scoff at me. This went on throughout most of my teenaged life. I wouldn't participate in sports in school, cheer, or anything that required being seen. I began to dim my light out of fear of being judged and dropped out of college. I vividly recall my first semester in college, during which I took an English course. The first assignment was a writing task, which I completed. But the day came to submit the paper, and the teacher called me first to read it out loud. I felt every eye in the room lock on me, my face burning with fear and embarrassment. I nervously protested aloud in a stern voice, "You didn't say anything about reading the paper in class!" The entire class turned to stare at me in disbelief. I shrank in my chair and responded, "I'm not ready," before hastily departing. And so began my long list of unfinished work. Fear of judgment had me in its merciless grasp until I had had enough.

You see that seemingly innocuous phrase "sticks and stones may break my bones, but words will never harm me" is, in fact, misleading. You can heal from the sticks and stones, but painful words filled with judgment can last a lifetime, robbing you of life! The phrase is often used to encourage children to ignore or brush off hurtful words or insults from others, emphasizing that physical harm is more impactful than verbal harm. However, in reality, words can significantly impact someone's mental and emotional well-being, and the phrase doesn't accurately reflect the effects Of verbal abuse. It's important to note that although the words might have been well-intentioned to build resilience in children, it's not an effective or helpful way to cope with verbal abuse. We must take verbal abuse seriously.

1

Chapter One - Understanding the Fear of Judgment.

8 steps from freedom -Breaking free from the fear of judgment

The fear of judgment casts a daunting shadow over many aspects of life, hindering personal growth and beyond. This trepidation may take on countless forms for men and women, ranging from self-doubt to societal pressures.

The apprehension of being judged is ubiquitous when we feel that others are negatively evaluating our actions. It wields tremendous influence over our internal state of mind and how we act and can profoundly affect our well-being. The roots of this fear are intricate and can stem from various causes.

One of the predominant factors contributing to the fear of judgment is social conditioning. From an early age, we learn to conform to society's expectations and seek validation from those around us. Unfortunately, this conditioning can lead to the development of an intense fear of judgment such that we believe even the slightest mistake or slip-up could lead to social isolation or rejection.

Another factor contributing to this fear is past experiences of criticism or rejection, which can be incredibly potent during childhood or adolescence when social skills and self-image develop.

The effects it has on women:

- **Appearance:** Women, ensnared by the critical gaze of others on their physical form, confront apprehensions surrounding body image and self-worth. This uneasiness is magnified by societal dictates that impose unyielding beauty ideals.
- **Motherhood:** In their role as nurturers, women often bear the weight of external scrutiny concerning their parenting choices. Each aspect invites unwarranted judgment, from decisions regarding breastfeeding or formula feeding to striking a work-life equilibrium.
- **Relationships:** The fear of judgment can have a profound impact on a woman's relationships, manifesting itself in a variety of ways. It may compel her to excessively worry about how her partner perceives her, causing her deep self-doubt and insecurity. In addition, this fear can impede her from expressing her genuine emotions and desires and establishing reasonable boundaries within the relationship, all for the sake of avoiding judgment or rejection. Furthermore, women can experience pressure to conform to cultural expectations of a "perfect" relationship, leaving them feeling inadequate or like failures if their partnership

doesn't match those norms. This fear may also inhibit women from seeking unconventional partners who fail to meet social standards. To surmount this fear, it is critical for women to develop self-acceptance and self-love and to prioritize their own needs and well-being in their relationships.

- **Personal Convictions:** The fear of judgment can significantly affect a woman's convictions in various ways. It may hinder her from expressing her thoughts and emotions or pursuing her passions and aspirations. Women may also feel pressured to conform to societal expectations and norms and constantly worry about being judged or criticized for deviating from these expectations. Such apprehension can cause a lack of self-confidence and self-worth, ultimately contributing to a sense of disconnect from one's true self. Women may feel they are living unauthentic or unfulfilling lives, which they perceive as devoid of purpose and meaning.

The effect it has on men:

- **Appearance:** The fear of judgment can affect men in various ways regarding appearance. Men may feel pressure to conform to societal standards of masculinity, including expectations around physical appearance. This can manifest in several ways, such as feeling self-conscious about their body shape or size, hair loss, skin imperfections, or aging. The fear of judgment around appearance can impact a man's self-esteem, confidence, and overall well-being. It can lead to feelings of inadequacy, shame, and anxiety. In addition, it can sometimes lead to more serious mental health issues, such as body dysmorphia or eating disorders.
- **Fatherhood:** Men may also feel judged or criticized by others for their parenting choices, whether how they discipline their children, how much time they spend with them, or other aspects of their parenting style. This fear of judgment can harm men's

mental health, well-being, and relationship with their children. Men may feel anxious or stressed about their ability to parent "correctly" and struggle with feelings of inadequacy, guilt, or shame if they fall short. This can also lead to a sense of disconnection or distance from their children, as they may feel unsure of how to connect with them or worry about being judged by others.

- **Relationships:** Men may feel immense pressure to conform to societal expectations of what it means to be a "good" or "masculine" partner, which can result in feelings of inadequacy or shame if they fall short of those expectations. Such pressure can manifest in different ways, such as feeling self-conscious about their appearance, financial situation, or sexual performance. Additionally, men may experience judgment or criticism from their partner or others regarding their behavior or choices in the relationship, thus creating unnecessary tension or conflict. A man may, for instance, feel judged by his partner for being emotional or vulnerable or criticized for failing to be "romantic" or attentive enough. These fears can severely impact men's self-esteem, mental health, and overall well-being, leading to difficulties in effective communication and building deep, emotional connections with their partners due to the fear of being judged or rejected. To overcome the fear of judgment in relationships, it is crucial for men to work on building their self-confidence and self-worth and to prioritize open and honest communication with their partners. Men can also challenge their internalized beliefs about gender roles and expectations in relationships and work towards developing a more authentic and fulfilling partnership based on mutual respect and understanding.

- **Personal Convictions:** The fear of judgment can impede a man's personal convictions or values, preventing him from expressing his actual beliefs or pursuing his passions. Men may experience pressure to conform to cultural norms or expectations and worry about being criticized for expressing opinions or beliefs that differ from those considered mainstream. This anxiety can result in a lack of self-expression and disconnection from one's true self. Thus, men may feel like they are living a life that is not genuine or satisfying, struggling to find significance or purpose in their pursuits. This fear can stem from factors such as societal expectations, negative past experiences, or a lack of self-confidence. Fear of judgment, or social anxiety, is an experience of deep discomfort that arises in social situations where individuals believe they may be evaluated or scrutinized by others. This fear, if not addressed, can lead to avoidance of certain activities or situations and can cause physical symptoms, such as sweating, trembling, and a rapid heart rate. Individuals that suffer from a fear of judgment often worry about being perceived as inadequate or that they may embarrass themselves in front of others. This fear can become so intense that it impedes their ability to function in everyday life and can cause them to isolate themselves from social situations. It is important to note that fear of judgment is common for many individuals, and proven treatments are available to help them manage and eventually overcome their fears.

When both partners struggle with the fear of judgment, it can create a dynamic where both parties are overly concerned with how they come across to each other. This can foster a cycle of self-doubt and insecurity and make communicating with one another openly and honestly much harder. In some cases, couples may find themselves caught up in constantly seeking validation from one another, which can lead to frustration and disappointment if their partner cannot provide the level of reassurance they desire.

To break this cycle, couples may benefit from working together to cultivate a shared sense of self-acceptance and self-love. This can involve setting mutual goals for personal growth and self-improvement and creating a supportive and encouraging environment where each partner feels safe to express their feelings and needs without fear of judgment.

Couples can also build their communication skills, including active listening and constructive feedback, which can help them navigate challenging conversations and resolve conflicts in a respectful and non-judgmental.

Ultimately, couples must approach their partnership with a deep commitment to each other's growth and well-being. Rather than imposing unrealistic expectations or demands, they should celebrate and capitalize on each other's unique strengths and qualities, creating a sense of mutual respect and understanding that can overcome any fear of judgment. By doing so, they can cultivate a relationship that is not only strong but also fulfilling, supporting and uplifting each other as they navigate through life's challenges and joys.

The fear of judgment can devastate oneself, leading to poor choices in relationships, as I know all too well. At 30, after a series of failed relationships, I thought I had finally escaped the cycle of choosing the wrong men. But then, on a sunny Saturday afternoon, as I was pumping gas, a voice called out to me, using the company of a child to gather my attention. He seemed harmless enough, so I let my guard down and conversed. This chance encounter led to the exchange of phone numbers. At the time, I was not in the best emotional or physical state; recovering from a minor surgery had weakened me, and now an intestinal virus had me feeling depleted. Conversations with this new-found suitor were therefore limited. Several days later, when he called, I told him I was not up for talking due to feeling ill. We hung up the phone, but an hour later, an unexpected knock was at my door. Weak and bleary-eyed, I approached the front door and asked the stranger how can I help him. He offered me an over-the-counter pain reliever and said, "I thought you might require these." Little did I know this seemingly kindly gesture would lead to a painful and transformative realization.

As I tried to understand how he found me, he offered a flimsy excuse. Despite feeling hesitant, I tried to maintain politeness and expressed my gratitude. As expected, he called me later and eventually asked me out. While some of me were still irked by his intrusion, I accepted his invitation. Initially, the outing was delightful, but he exhibited furious and peculiar behavior when I attempted to leave. I was taken aback; it was just a date, and I had been eager to return to my own home. I calmly insisted on going, got in my car, and drove home, ready to sleep. Little did I know that my *peace* would be disturbed by a loud banging on my door at an ungodly hour the following day. I groggily went to the front door and saw that he was wearing the same, now wrinkled, green printed shirt from our date. Despite my irritation and sharp tone, he apologized and asked permission to come in to talk. Against my better judgment, I let him into my living room, and as he began to share his life story of substance abuse, I kindly expressed that I would drop him back at his mother's house, for this was not an experience I wished to have. So, after retrieving some outerwear, we set off for his home. The entire trip was marked with sincere apologies on his part. Upon arrival, I made a decision I later regretted - I declined his invitation to meet his mother. However, after feeling guilty for her earlier help in providing me with some pain reliever for my physical ailment, I went inside to speak with her. Understandably, her reaction to my morning encounter with her son was disgusted.

Meanwhile, he had gone off for a quick shower and asked that I not leave. Although hesitant, I reluctantly remained. He then requested we walk to the nearby playground to discuss his soul's burdens, and, though skeptical, I acceded to his request. As we sat there, he divulged his innermost thoughts and feelings about his past mishaps and experiences of being alone. Lo and behold, I resonated with this sensation of loneliness. Despite the myriad of red flags, my desire to be his support and please him outweighed any rational thought I had remaining. My initial inclination was to flee, but my propensity to put others before myself won the day. After he vowed never to use drugs again, he began to show signs of a caring, compassionate man. My weakened defenses allowed him entrance into my life and, even more alarmingly, around my two children. However, his demeanor eventually changed from caring to cruel, and the person who emerged from behind that veil of deceit became my dreadful abuser.

I endured four excruciating years at the hands of my once kind suitor, a period wherein I could not even recognize who I had become. Suffering with only the sounds of my weeping as a witness, I bore the brunt of physical, emotional, mental, verbal, and sexual abuse from someone who claimed to love me - - even after every beating. Every day, I would cover up my shame, pain, and embarrassment, and appear well-put-together, showing up strong in the church, where all eyes were constantly on me. The fear of another public humiliation was too much to handle, especially as a mother of two who had divorced and was now living with another man -- what they called "shacking up." Life with my suitor was hell, one I had to cover up due to shame and fear of being judged again! I had failed in two marriages prior -- the truth being, I didn't marry for love. I married because "I was a PK," and the perception and judgment from everyone around me were un-acceptable. So, to save face, I married -- but deep inside, I knew I could not marry my suitor, no matter what anyone said or thought, because I had to draw the line.

During the last six months of that excruciatingly painful relation-ship, I embarked on a journey of self-discovery and self-worth. Every morning after my kids left for school, I devoted myself to prayer, medi-tation, writing, and worship and gradually began to glimpse the stirring of my inner power. I realized, with mounting clarity, that for my own sake and my children's, I needed to free myself from this unbearable situation. I began to share my anguish with strangers - after all, they couldn't judge me, or so I believed. Finally, one morning, while sob-bing on my knees, I cried out to God for help. With stunning clarity, I heard His voice respond: "You've been talking to everyone else about what to do, but have you ever asked me?" Then came the question, "If I offer you a way out, will you take it?" I answered in the affirmative. For two weeks, I wondered when and how my escape would present itself. Then, one Sunday after church, it arrived - but in the form of a brutal beating, to the point of being kicked to the ground and having spit hawked in my face from five feet away. All the while, my then approximately nine-year-old child was downstairs, hearing the screams and cries of his helpless mother.

As I dragged myself to the shower, tears streaming down my face, I let out a sound I had never heard before. It echoed through the empty walls of my home, a cry from deep within my soul that sounded like a war cry. And at that moment, I felt a surge of strength unlike any I had ever experienced.

I dressed quickly, my suitor lying lazily across my bed, and picked up the cordless phone. Slowly, I descended the stairs, my heart pounding with trepidation. My child sat there, tense and unresponsive, refusing to meet my gaze. I called him several times before he finally turned to face me. And then I said the words I had dreaded that would change everything: "It's over."

I called my mother and siblings, telling them everything that had happened relieved to finally have their support. While I was on the phone, my oldest son called from work. He heard my voice's pain and immediately knew something was wrong. "Ma," he asked, "are you okay? Did he hurt you?" I assured him that I was alright, that it was over. And as I hung up the phone, I felt a sense of overwhelming relief.

Before I knew it, my townhouse was filled with police and family members, their concern and kindness palpable. At that moment, I no longer cared what anyone thought of me. I had done what was best for me and my children, and I felt alive for the first time in a long time.

A few days after his arrest, I received a call from the House of Ruth, a home for women who had experienced abuse. The voice on the other end was gentle and kind, introducing herself and sharing the reason for her call. And although I lashed out defensively, saying that I was not a victim of anything, I knew deep down that she was right. I had been through so much, and it was time to start healing.

I spent many years of my life cloaked in shame for my choices. I lived in terror of my abuser and the unkind words others might say. I was afraid of being alone, of being looked down upon, and of being laughed at once more. These fears consumed me, but there was not enough self-love or self-worth to counteract them. So instead, I chose to live in a cycle of abuse rather than face the harsh opinions of others. In my mind, being treated like I was worthless was better than being considered weak by those who thought they knew me. The fear of judgment consumed me entirely, eroding my sense of self-worth, until one day, I realized that I was worth so much more than that.

The terror of judgment can contribute to domestic violence in many ways. Sometimes, you may experience profound disgrace, remorse, or trepidation of being judged by others for being caught in an abusive relationship. This fear can impede victims from seeking help or support and make them feel trapped or isolated.

In other cases, an individual may manipulate and control their partner using the fear of judgment. For instance, they may threaten to divulge personal information or shame their partner in front of others if they disobey their requirements. This may cause a cycle of abuse and control as victims feel increasingly trapped and powerless.

It is necessary to comprehend that domestic violence is a multifaceted issue with numerous underlying causes, and the fear of judgment is just one of the multiple factors that can contribute to it. Domestic violence should never be taken lightly, and if you know of anyone or you are a victim, it is imperative to immediately seek help. Addressing domestic violence necessitates a comprehensive approach that includes education, awareness, prevention, and intervention at all levels of society.

The Root and its Development.

The fear of judgment is a complex phenomenon from genetic and environmental factors. Some individuals may develop the fear of judgment due to early-life experiences or traumatic events, such as bullying or humiliation. Additionally, social learning theory suggests that individuals may learn to fear judgment by observing others being criticized or judged in social situations. Ultimately, the development of the fear of judgment is likely influenced by various contributing factors.

The dread of censure is an omnipresent human emotion that arises from the perception of unfavorable criticism. It has the power to mold our thoughts, feelings, and actions and can impact our mental health and overall well-being. The roots of this dread are complicated and may have originated from a multiplicity of sources.

Social conditioning is one of the primary sources of experiencing this type of dread. From an early age, we are taught to comply with social norms and seek recognition and acceptance from others. Unfortunately, this conditioning can lead us to develop an intense fear of criticism resulting in social exclusion or isolation.

Past experiences of rejection or criticism can also significantly contribute to developing this emotion. For example, adverse experiences during childhood or adolescence - when we build our sense of self and social skills, can result in an unwavering belief that we are inferior and persistently fear the judgment of others.

Cultural factors can also play a role in the fear of criticism. For example, some cultures emphasize conformity, stigmatize exposure of discomforting personal information, and emphasize the avoidance of shame or embarrassment. These cultural factors intensify anxiety and apprehension toward being judged by others.

Lastly, individual factors such as temperament and personality traits can also contribute to the dread of negative criticism. For example, individuals prone to anxiety or self-doubt may be more susceptible to the fear of judgment. Understanding these roots can help construct strategies to overcome or manage the fear of criticism, building greater self-confidence and resilience.

Identifying the culprit

1. When did you first start feeling judged or criticized by others?

   ____

   How did it leave you feeling?

   ____

2. Are there any past experiences or traumas that have contributed to your fear of judgement?

   ____

3. Have you noticed any patterns in the situations or people that trigger your fear of judgement?

   ____

4. Do you feel like your fear of judgement is rooted in a particular area of your life, such as relationships, work, or appearance?

   ____

5. Have you ever received feedback or criticism that you found particularly difficult to accept or move past?

   ____

6. How do you typically respond to situations that trigger your fear of judgement? Do you avoid them, confront them, or try to ignore them?

   ____

7. Have you noticed any negative self-talk or limiting beliefs that contribute to your fear of judgement?

   ____

8. What would it mean to you to overcome your fear of judgement, and how would your life be different if you were able to do so?

   ____

2

Chapter Two - Overcoming Negative Self-Talk and Limiting Beliefs

Negative self-talk, which relates to the fear of being judged, can be described as the critical inner voice or negative thoughts that one holds about themselves concerning the opinions or expectations of others. This thought pattern involves a strong focus on one's perceived flaws, inadequacies, and mistakes while simultaneously assuming that others harshly judge or view them negatively. When left unchecked, negative self-talk can be highly detrimental to one's self-esteem and level of confidence, leading to increased anxiety, self-doubt, and avoidance behaviors. Such self-talk can manifest in expressions such as "I'm not good enough," "What will people think of me?" or "I can't possibly do this."

Identifying and challenging negative internal conversations and limiting beliefs is essential to improving your mental health and well-being. Here are some steps that can be helpful in this process:

1. The first step in challenging negative self-talk and the limitations of your beliefs is to become aware of them. Take time to observe the thoughts that pass through your mind throughout the day

and how they make you feel. Negative self-talk often involves ideas that are critical, judgmental, or self-defeating. What are you saying to yourself? How do you describe yourself? Is the first thought that visits your mind positive or negative?

I grew up in a house of faith built on fear for years. Conversations were often wrapped in fear, such as "every time something good happens, something bad is around the corner," which made me afraid of being happy because bad things happen to good people. Negative thoughts, however, often plagued my thinking, despite my desire to be satisfied. I heard negative conversations, from every superstition to fear of exploring life and taking chances, and I learned to talk myself out of anything. Negative words and thoughts are like being suffocated in a world of darkness, never realizing that all you need to do is switch on the light, and night will disappear. Take time to notice yourself and your daily thoughts. Do you lean towards negative conversations or love hearing about others' struggles? What thoughts run through your mind about how people see you? Do you imagine the glass as half empty or half full? Do you believe that there is always someone better than you for the position, that you are not marriage-worthy? Your thinking determines how you show up. So, do you think that "shit happens to everyone," or do you believe that "every day, there is an expectation that great things will happen for me?"

2. Challenge and transform your thoughts: Once you've identified the negative self-talk and limiting beliefs that hold you back, challenge them. Ask yourself if they are based on facts or assumptions, if they are rational or irrational if they help or harm you. For instance, if you have the thought, "I always mess up everything I do," seek to replace it with one that's more empowering and accurate, such as "I have had challenges in the past, but they do not define me. I possess the capacity to learn and grow." Never allow a setback or a challenge to determine your worth or value.

3. Cultivate a mindset of positivity and self-love: After confronting and transforming your negative self-talk, transform it into more positive and self-affirming thoughts. Rather than thinking, "I'm a failure," for example, reframe it into something like, "I've had setbacks, but they don't define me. I am deserving of great things and cultivating meaningful relationships."

Cultivating a mindset of positivity and self-love requires a dedicated commitment, yet it is a worthy investment in your mental and emotional well-being. Here are some strategies that can help to aid in this effort:

- **Empower your soul with self-care:** Engage in activities that nourish and lift your spirit, whether relishing in the beauty of nature, practicing mindfulness, or engaging in enlightening conversations with cherished friends. When we place self-care at the forefront of our priorities, we demonstrate to ourselves that we deserve the divine gifts of love and care.
- **Cultivate a more positive mindset:** Shift your attention to gratitude. Dwell on the things you are thankful for no matter how small they may seem. This daily practice will guide your thoughts away from negativity and towards positivity.
- **Challenge their negative self-talk:** As we discussed previously, negative self-talk can harm our overall mental well-being. Therefore, reframing these negative thoughts into more positive ones is a beneficial practice.
- **Surround yourself with positivity:** Surround yourself with individuals who elevate and enrich your spirit and are a source of encouragement and support. Consciously allocate your time and energy towards those who uplift you and bring positivity into your life. Conversely, it is vital to limit the amount of exposure you have to individuals who drain your energy or exude negativity. Remember, the people you associate with can

significantly impact your emotional and mental well-being. So, strive to surround yourself with those who bring out the best in you and help you to shine your brightest.

- **Embrace imperfection:** Embrace the imperfection inherent in the human experience. Grant yourself the freedom to commit errors, as they serve as valuable opportunities for growth, rather than indulging in excessive self-criticism. Give yourself the gift of grace.
- **Set positive affirmations:** Generate a roster of empowering declarations that resonate with your innermost being and recite them frequently. For instance, "I am deserving of affection and admiration or I possess the capability to actualize my ambitions."
- **Celebrate your successes:** It is essential to take a moment to celebrate your achievements, no matter how insignificant they may appear. Doing so can empower your self-assurance and reinforce the practice of nurturing your inner voice with positive thoughts.
- **Live your life with gratitude:** Every day, find something to be thankful for. Take a moment to express your gratitude - whether it's towards God, your parents, teachers, spouse, or kids. By cultivating an attitude of thankfulness, we unlock the exquisite beauty of the little things that make life worth living. With diligent practice and perseverance, one can cultivate a mindset rooted in positivity and self-love. This involves a commitment to self-care, regularly expressing gratitude for the blessings in life, challenging the toxic tendrils of negative self-talk, nurturing a circle of positivity, embracing imperfection with grace, setting affirmative intentions, and allowing space to honor achievements both big and small. These tried-and-true strategies can usher in a new era of internal growth, resilience, and overall well-being.

4. It is imperative to cultivate self-compassion. Practicing self-compassion is absolutely crucial. As you challenge your negative self-talk and limiting beliefs, you must be kinder and more compassionate towards yourself. It is critical to recognize that everyone encounters negative thoughts from time to time, and it is normal to experience self-doubt and insecurity. Despite this being normal, it is essential not to habitually question yourself or your abilities. Instead, when you feel yourself struggling, take a moment to find reasons to praise your unique qualities and strengths. Remember, dear one, that you hold the key to success. No external force or obstacle can hinder your journey toward your highest potential; only your self-doubt and fears can hold you back. So let go of any limiting beliefs and trust in your innate strength, for the universe is conspiring in your favor.

Additionally, consider seeking sustenance from an esteemed confidant, a family member, a life coach, or a mental health practitioner who can equip you with further stratagems and methodologies to combat your negative self-talk and self-limiting beliefs. In sum, identifying and disputing negative self-talk and self-limiting beliefs involves recognizing your thoughts, contesting them, substituting them with affirmative ones, practicing self-kindness, and seeking sustenance. With diligence, you can cultivate a more inspiring and empowering mindset to ameliorate your mental health and overall well-being.

Strategies for reframing negative thoughts and building a more positive self-image:

1. **Be aware of your negative self-talk:** Observe the moments when your inner voice criticizes or doubts you and record them. This enables you to recognize recurring patterns and triggers and equip yourself against them.

2. **Reframe negative thoughts:** With a simple shift in mindset, negative thoughts can transform into powerful affirmations. Rather than claiming "I can't do this," embrace the possibility of growth by saying, "I am capable of learning how to do this." This

change in perspective allows you to unlock your full potential and discover the limitless opportunities that await you.

3. **Incorporate empowering affirmations into your daily routine:** Take the time to write down positive affirmations that invoke self-love, worth, and strength. Repeat these empowering messages to yourself frequently throughout the day. For example, embrace thoughts like "I am enough, ""I am worthy of love and respect," and "I possess the strength to overcome any obstacle."

4. **Embrace the practice of gratitude and allow it to manifest in your life:** Take a moment to acknowledge the abundance surrounding you; ponder the things you are thankful for, big and small. In these moments of reflection, shift your focus to the positivity in your reality. As you cultivate appreciation, allow it to permeate the deepest parts of your being, and watch as it transforms your life.

Dare to upend your self-imposed constraints and shatter the limiting beliefs that constrict your potential. Take the first step towards liberation by identifying these beliefs that have long held you back. For example, if the insidious narrative you harbor is whispering that you are unworthy of the esteemed promotion at work, confront it by challenging its veracity. Is it genuinely valid? Courageously ask yourself this question and revel in the liberation of demolishing these self-defeating notions. Practice self-compassion: Be gentle and compassionate towards yourself. Recognize that everyone makes mistakes and has flaws and that it is okay to be imperfect.2. Imagine achieving the success you crave: Envision yourself conquering the challenges that currently vex you. This powerful practice can bolster your self-assurance and foster a radiant self-image.

Surround yourself with a flourishing garden of positivity by surrounding yourself with positive and supportive individuals who uplift you, affirm your worth, and catalyze your growth. This creates a cycle of reinforcing positive self-talk, cultivating a more wholesome and nourishing self-image, and radiating more joy, kindness, and compassion to all beings. Let this circle of light expand outward and envelop your life, illuminating every corner with vibrant colors of hope, inspiration, and love.

Identifying Negative Self-Talk

Instructions:

Take a few moments to reflect on your thoughts and feelings about yourself. Write down any negative thoughts that come to mind, no matter how small or insignificant they may seem. For each negative thought, ask yourself the following questions and write down your answers:

- Is this thought based on fact or assumption?
- Where did this thought come from? (e.g., past experiences, societal messages, personal beliefs)
- What evidence do I have to support or contradict this thought?
- How does this thought make me feel?
- How does this thought affect my behavior and actions?
- Is this thought helpful or harmful to me?
- What would I say to a friend who had this same thought?
- How can I reframe this thought into something more positive and empowering?

- After answering these questions, take a moment to reflect on any patterns or themes that emerge from your negative self-talk. Use this worksheet as a tool to help you identify and challenge your negative self-talk and replace it with more positive and empowering thoughts.

Negative Thought #1:

____

Is this thought based on fact or assumption?

____

Where did this thought come from?

____

What evidence do I have to support or contradict this thought?

____

How does this thought make me
feel?____

How does this thought affect my behavior and
actions?____

 Is this thought helpful or harmful to me?

____

What would I say to a friend who had this same thought?

____

How can I reframe this thought into something more positive and
empowering?

____

3

Chapter Three - Building Self-Awareness and Self-Acceptance

Developing self-awareness and mindfulness is critical to overcoming the fear of judgment. Self-awareness involves being aware of one's thoughts, emotions, and behaviors, while mindfulness is the practice of being fully present at the moment and accepting things without judgment. For years, I merely existed, and my daily thoughts were scattered. I lacked control because I accepted all conscious or unconscious thoughts as the truth of who I was. Much to my displeasure, I later learned many of those negative thoughts were learned behavioral and thought patterns or negative self-talk implanted by the fear and negativity I had experienced.

I was oblivious to my true self and identity, merely existing in a world of self-doubt. However, on one particular birthday, when I was in my fifties, my husband and I went on a day trip, and it was during that excursion that realization hit me like an avalanche. I had never lived my own life! My life was a reflection of the thoughts, beliefs, and judgments of others. I lived in the shadow of others' limitations and belief systems, so I barely lived at all. That moment sparked an intense desire to become self-aware, to discover who I was, what I thought, what I loved, and what I aspired to become. I yearned to know who the true me was. Thus, the quest began taking a new journey.

By developing mindfulness and self-awareness, you, too, can recognize and manage the fear of judgment. Start today by being mindful of your daily thoughts. Ask yourself, "Are these my thoughts or someone else's?" Then learn to live in the moment with yourself, with your thoughts and desires, relishing everything that makes you uniquely you.

Thus began my next journey toward self-discovery - an ardent quest to unveil my innate passions and aspirations beneath the myriad layers of external influence. Embracing the journey toward authenticity demanded discerning mindfulness in every thought encountered: were these reflections genuinely mine or merely echoes of others? It was crucial to cultivate a connection with each moment, thought, and desire - irrespective of its nature - celebrating those quintessential elements which defined my singularity. By fostering these essential attributes within myself, I acquired unparalleled mastery in recognizing and managing the pervasive fear of judgment.

One way to develop self-awareness is the practice of introspection. Make a daily effort to reflect deeply on your innermost thoughts and emotions. Notice when negative self-talk arises and try to reframe those thoughts more positively.

This can help you to recognize and skillfully manage negative patterns of thinking and portraying emotions, which can often act as a potent trigger for fear of judgment.

Another way to develop self-awareness is to be attuned to your bodily sensations. It is imperative to take heed of times when you feel tense or uncomfortable and make an effort to identify their root cause. By doing so, triggers that spur feelings of judgment, such as certain individuals or circumstances, can be identified.

Practicing mindfulness can prove beneficial in overcoming the fear of judgment by enabling you to be fully present at the moment and learn acceptance of things as they are without allowing judgment to cloud your mind. This practice helps you release your concerns regarding the future or remorse about the past, which can be regular sources of anxiety and apprehension.

To practice mindfulness, try to focus on your breath and the sensations in your body. Notice when your mind begins to wander, and gently bring your attention back to the present moment. This can help to calm your mind and reduce anxiety.

By cultivating self-awareness and mindfulness, one can transcend the fear of judgment. Through introspection, being attuned to physical sensations, and attentiveness to the present moment, we can develop the discernment to identify and regulate negative thoughts and emotions while shedding worries over the future and regrets of the past. With continued practice, these methods can bolster our resilience and confidence, insulating us from the heavy-handed influence of the fear of judgment in our everyday lives.

Embrace

The power tool of self-acceptance and self-compassion for building confidence

Embracing self-acceptance and self-compassion involves acknowledging our flaws and imperfections while recognizing our inherent worth as individuals. It means treating ourselves kindly and compassionately, just as we would with a dear friend or loved one. Taking the time to study and know oneself leads to a sense of gratitude.

I often take new mothers on an emotional journey of appreciation, encouraging them to look in the mirror at their newly formed bodies and thank themselves for not giving up, for staying the course, and for providing a safe and nurturing home to their bundle of joy. After all, their bodies are the gateways of life to their children and are worth praising.

Sometimes we must set internal reminder clocks and remind ourselves with an appreciation of all the things our bodies have endured and how we've continued to get up and press on. Being kind to ourselves may not always feel good, but it is good for our souls. We all have our imperfections, but they don't define us. You are more than the sum of all your findings. You are a remarkable being made up of greatness, intelligence, and grace, and you are worth it all!

Self-acceptance and self-compassion are formidable tools for cultivating confidence. They aid in redirecting our gaze from our shortcomings to our strengths and uplifting qualities. When we exhibit self-kindness and self-compassion, we more frequently visualize our future selves as successful, overcome adversity with ease, and manifest our aspirations into reality.

When we embrace and accept ourselves with self-compassion, we can significantly diminish the impact of negative self-talk and self-criticism, the two significant sources of anxiety and self-doubt. By acknowledging our worth and treating ourselves with tenderness, we can alleviate feelings of shame, guilt, and unworthiness and foster a more optimistic and empowering mindset.

Self-acceptance and self-compassion can fortify us to evolve resilience in the face of setbacks and challenges. When we treat ourselves with benevolence and empathy, we better grasp stress and adversities and rebound from impediments with rejuvenated determination and confidence.

In essence, embracing self-acceptance and self-compassion translates to treating ourselves with tender kindness, genuine care, and profound understanding and wholeheartedly accepting ourselves for who we indeed are. It represents a potent tool for cultivating immeasurable self-confidence, enabling us to shift our focus towards our inherent strengths and positive attributes, gradually mitigating negative and self-critical self-narrative, and fostering an indomitable spirit that can brave through tumultuous trials. By consciously practicing self-acceptance and self-compassion, we can develop an unshakeable sense of self-worth and an unparalleled and unquantifiable self-assurance that empowers us to live more satisfying, gratifying, and meaningful lives as we become more in tune with our intrinsic selves as well as more enlightened and spiritually aligned beings.

Embracing Yourself

Instructions: Take some time to reflect on the following questions and write down your answers. Use these questions as a guide to help you embrace and appreciate yourself more fully.

1. What are your unique strengths and qualities?

   ____

2. What are some accomplishments you are proud of?

   ____

3. How do you take care of yourself physically, emotionally, and mentally______________________________________

4. What brings you joy and happiness?

____

5. What are some things you can do to practice self-care and   self-compassion? ____

6. What are some things you can do to honor and celebrate your uniqueness? ____

7. How can you show yourself more kindness and understanding?

   ____

8. What are some positive affirmations you can say to yourself to boost your self-esteem?

Reflection: Take a moment to reflect on your answers. What insights did you gain from this exercise? _

What actions can you take to continue embracing yourself?

Remember to be patient and kind to yourself as you continue on this journey.

4

Chapter Four - Cultivating Resilience and Adaptability

Resilience is the art of adaptation and the strength to rise from challenging and arduous situations. It encompasses the capacity to confront hardship, overcome barriers, and sustain hope and positivity amidst setbacks and failures. It's not about circumventing or doing away with challenges. *Instead*, it's about nurturing and honing the skills and resources to tackle them head-on. The *resilient* spring forth in the face of adversities with a positive disposition and leverage their strengths and resources to navigate testing circumstances.

Situations and circumstances may emerge to derail you, but resilience enables you to stay afloat despite appearances. This is because the resilient have a deep strength within themselves, much like a skilled surfer who maintains their balance and rides the powerful waves.

Resilience is not a fixed trait but a skill that can be developed and strengthened over time. It involves building a solid support network, practicing self-care and self-compassion, developing problem-solving skills, and cultivating a positive mindset.

Resilience is a crucial virtue as it enables us to navigate through trying times effectively with an unshakable sense of hope and optimism. Furthermore, it allows us to recover from setbacks and failures and learn from those experiences in a way that helps us evolve and grow as individuals.

Being resilient means possessing the fortitude to adapt and rebound from daunting circumstances. It involves honing skills and resources to contend with obstacles, sustaining a constructive outlook, and fostering a sturdy support network. Resilience is crucial as it empowers us to manage stress and adversity, rebound from setbacks, and evolve and thrive as individuals.

"The key to resilience is not simply observing the present situation, but maintaining an unwavering focus on the intended outcome."

Building resilience and adaptability

In a constantly changing and unpredictable world, it is essential to develop resilience and adaptability. Life can throw unexpected challenges and obstacles our way, and how we handle these situations define our character. When you are resilient, you can bounce back from setbacks, learn from failures, and persevere through difficult times. The ability to be adaptable you can adjust to new situations and environments, remain flexible in the face of change, and stay proactive instead of reactive. We can lead a more fulfilling and successful life by cultivating these qualities within ourselves. Let us embrace the opportunities for growth and transformation that life presents us and become stronger from them.

Steps to building resilience and adaptability:

1. **Develop your growth mindset** by opening your mind to endless possibilities. A growth mindset acknowledges the immense power of effort and learning in transforming our abilities and

skills. Rather than viewing challenges as insurmountable obstacles, we see them as fertile grounds for personal growth and learning. Embracing a growth mindset can propel us towards greater positivity and resilience that help us thrive in unfamiliar and adverse situations and rise above setbacks. It's all about how you see things from your perspective. One's perspective shapes their entire perception of reality. It is a fundamental aspect of how we understand and experience the world around us. By cultivating a spiritual lens through which to view the world, we can unlock more profound levels of meaning and insight and begin to appreciate the beauty and interconnectedness of all things.

2. **Build a Support System:** Creating and nurturing a solid support system of genuine and caring friends, family, and colleagues is vital for developing our resilience and adaptability to life's challenges. Our support system provides a sense of community, belonging, and security to help us cope with stress and adversity. When we build solid relationships and seek support when needed, we strengthen our inner resources, cultivate emotional intelligence, and develop a deep sense of trust and compassion.

3. **The practice of self-care** is an essential aspect of building resilience and adaptability. It involves prioritizing our physical, mental, and emotional well-being, which can be achieved through ample sleep, proper exercise, and nutritious meals. Making time for activities that fill us with joy and relaxation is equally essential, nurturing our spirit and overall vitality.

4. **Strengthening our capacity** to recognize difficulties and devise solutions is crucial to cultivating resilience and versatility. As you enhance your aptitude for problem-solving skills, you can boost your confidence and proficiency in surmounting obstacles and adversities with graceful adeptness.

5. **Embrace adversity:** Rather than viewing setbacks as failures, perceive them as opportunities for growth and enlightenment. Through self-reflection and learning from your mistakes, you can

cultivate new skills and approaches that can aid you in adapting to unfamiliar circumstances and rising to meet future challenges with greater ease and confidence. In life, we constantly learn and grow or teach and inspire others. So when faced with adversity, don't interpret it as a failure; see it as a tool to learn from and use to advance to your next level. Learning and growing is a life-long process that involves developing new skills, gaining knowledge, and expanding our perspectives. Whether we consciously acknowledge it or not, we are always in the process of learning and growing. It's just sometimes the lessons are felt more intensely. At the same time, we can teach and inspire others to learn and grow. By sharing the knowledge, experiences, and insights learned through our failures, we can help others develop their skills and abilities to reach their full potential.

Learning from failure and using it to grow and strengthen your confidence.

Learning lessons from our failures involves reflecting on our experiences, analyzing what went wrong, and using that knowledge to enhance our future performance. It consists in seeing failure not as a source of disgrace or defeat but as an opportunity for personal growth and enlightenment. By learning from our mistakes, we can gain valuable insights about ourselves, our strengths and weaknesses, and the best strategies for us. By recognizing what didn't work and why, we can cultivate new skills, techniques, and approaches that can help us to improve our performance and accomplish our objectives.

Learning from our mistakes can help to fortify our self-assurance. When we view failure as a chance for growth, we become less susceptible to disappointment caused by hindrances and more likely to push through any obstacles. By cultivating the resilience to recover from our failures, we can establish our confidence and develop a sensation of dominance and authority over our lives.

To extract wisdom from our mistakes, it is crucial to confront them with an attitude of learning. This requires reimagining our failures as opportunities for progress rather than as proof of our flaws or shortcomings. It similarly involves being receptive to feedback and willing to experiment with novel approaches and tactics.

In the fullness of our learning from that stage of development, we no longer consider our past mistakes as failures. Rather, they become important opportunities for **GREATER** advancements in our lives.

G - Growth mindset: Cultivate a growth mindset that sees failure as an opportunity for learning and growth.

R - Reflect: Take the time to reflect on your experiences and identify what went wrong and what you can learn from it.

E - Experiment: Be open to experimenting with new approaches and strategies to improve your performance.

A - Accept feedback: Be willing to accept feedback and constructive criticism as a means of improving your performance.

T - Take action: Use what you've learned to take action and improve your performance.

E - Embrace the journey: Remember that learning and growth are a journey, and that setbacks and failures are a natural part of that journey.

R - Reassess and adjust: Continuously reassess your progress and adjust your strategies as needed to keep moving forward.

"FAILURES ARE JUST OPPORTUNITIES FOR GROWTH AND ADVANCEMENTS "

Learning from failure entails taking the time to introspect on our experiences, identifying the factors that hindered our success, and harnessing that knowledge to enhance our future endeavors. By perceiving failure as an opportunity for growth and self-improvement, we can cultivate the fortitude and self-assurance essential for overcoming obstacles and realizing our ambitions.

"I just didn't' fall into success I learned my way to it"

5

Chapter Five - Strengthen Your Boundaries.

I often tell those whom I mentor and coach that I wish I had a mentor like myself back then, in those years when my life was a never-ending cycle of despair. Back then, I did not comprehend nor realize the significance of boundaries, so my existence was on an unceasing loop for decades. It wasn't until I stumbled upon my journey of transformation that the realization struck me. During that particular season, my husband and I were overseeing a church in one state while pastoring in another. Driven by our enormous hearts for people, we neglected to set boundaries in our personal and professional lives. As it happens with anything that lacks boundaries, eventually, everything will come crashing down upon oneself, and sometimes, it can either make or break you. As for us, our process broke us down before we could find a way back to remaking ourselves. I will never forget the anguish and endless tears that flowed from our souls when we were caught off guard and crushed. I remember lying on my bed, deep in thought, wondering how we ended up where we were, how we missed all the signs that were everywhere around us. With mornings of much prayer, meditation, worship, and writing, the answer came to me in a tender voice. "Because you allowed it," said the voice. My tears flowed even more fiercely as I asked, "What do you mean by 'we allowed it?'" Then came the revelation everything that happened to us was a result of what we allowed by not setting boundaries. We created a culture in our churches that treated everyone like they were a part of our immediate family, and we let both people and situations invade our intimate space, be it our homes or our lives. Instead of setting necessary boundaries out of the quiet fear of judgment, we brought them into our sacred spaces, our inner circle, which should have been reserved only for our family. We built a life where the church was our family, friends, and travel partners. Our entire lives revolved around the same people. Our conversations, our laughter, and ultimately, our tears were shared with the same group. So, when the unfortunate, unforeseen break-up surfaced, we were left with feelings of abandonment from every direction. During that next phase of subsequent self-discovery, as I was journaling, I was reminded that I, by giving everyone the power to do to me what was done, allowed them. That's when I penned my personal day off.

My personal day off

Today I choose to use this day as my personal day;
I close all doors that lead to distractions on my thoughts towards destiny,
I reject all words that becomes wounds in my thoughts,

I shut all eyes that search for openings in my soul
to track me in the secret place of mediation,

I erase all negative images of me that I accepted as my own,
While they were the visions of another's creation.

I release myself from the strongholds of shame and
guilt that has encaged my being,

I collapse all portals of access that leads to my heart;
I choose who gains access and relinquish the eagerness
to let pain be joined from the start.

Today, I rescue my peace that I allowed trouble to invade;
I reclaim my joy from the demand of my personal distractions.
Today, I close my mouth, reserve my opinion, occupy my own thoughts,
draw my own conclusion, dream my own dreams, visit my own life,
accept my own success, learn from my own failures, fill my own mind,
guard my own heart, and take advantage of my own time!
After all it's my personal day off
Now if you would excuse me for a moment while
I take others opinion of me off my back.
Now, that's a load I no longer carry because today I decided
It's My Personal Day Off.

Setting boundaries will not prevent the sting of betrayals, but it will undoubtedly provide an emotional cushion for the heart when the rug is yanked out from under you. In my journey of recovery and self-discovery, I realized that I can choose who enters my life and who I release, and it is solely up to me to establish those boundaries. It is not the fault of others for accessing parts of my life; I must take responsibility for granting them access. I have become a better and more robust version of myself by releasing the past and forgiving those who wronged me. This time, with clear and firm boundaries in place, I can move forward with confidence and integrity.

Learn to set boundaries and protect your self-esteem from negative influences.

- One of the most essential life skills is the ability to set healthy boundaries and safeguard your self-worth from toxic influences. This requires deep self-awareness, an unwavering commitment to your moral principles, and a fearless attitude toward those who try to undermine your confidence or manipulate your emotions. It means knowing when to say "no," when to assert your needs when to walk away from a harmful situation, and when to stand up for what you believe in. Finally, it means recognizing that your well-being matters just as much as anyone else's and that you deserve love, respect, and compassion no matter what. So, if you want to live a fulfilling and authentic life, start practicing the art of boundary-setting today, and watch as your inner strength and resilience grow stronger with every step.
- Setting boundaries is crucial for safeguarding our psychological and emotional health against negative influences. Essentially, applying limitations enables us to establish lucid limits regarding what we are and are not willing to tolerate while simultaneously communicating our expectations for how we wish to be treated.

Should we fail to enforce boundaries, we may encounter massive levels of overwhelm, stress, and resentment when attempting to satisfy the needs of others at our own expense. Eventually, we may even begin to doubt our self-worth and esteem as we start to assume that our welfare is neither essential nor worthy of consideration.

- Setting clear boundaries is essential to safeguarding one's self-esteem and mental well-being. By doing so, we prioritize our individual needs, principles, and beliefs, instilling a sense of empowerment and confidence in our dealings with others. More so, boundary-setting encourages positive and healthy relationships, fostering honest communication, genuine respect, and a supportive environment.When we fail to establish clear boundaries in our life, we expose ourselves to a host of detrimental effects that can adversely affect our mental and emotional health, relationships with others, and a general sense of well-being. Let's consider some examples:

- **Overcommitment**: In our eagerness to please, to appear co-operative and caring, we often agree to take on more than we can handle, extending ourselves beyond reasonable limits with no thought for our own physical, emotional, or mental health. Though this may seem like a selfless act, in truth, it can lead to weakened relationships, diminished productivity, and a general sense of malaise. The key, then, is to establish healthy personal boundaries that honor both ourselves and those whom we serve, which allows us to show up fully and joyfully, rather than frayed and depleted.

- **Resentment** can fester within us when we neglect to establish healthy boundaries. We may find ourselves growing increasingly resentful towards others who disregard our needs and take advantage of us. This unhealthy dynamic can cause our relationships to deteriorate, leading to negative emotions towards others and ourselves.

- **Low self-esteem** Without healthy boundaries, we might begin to question our own worth and significance, and even feel that our needs and desires are irrelevant or trivial. This can result in a diminished sense of self-esteem and a lack of confidence in our inherent abilities and potential. It is imperative to cultivate healthy boundaries in order to protect and nourish our sense of self-worth and self-respect.

- **Toxic relationships:** If we fail to establish healthy boundaries, we may inadvertently attract or accept toxic individuals in our lives. These individuals, sadly, do not possess our best interests at heart, and may engage in emotionally abusive or manipulative behaviors that can ultimately harm our mental and emotional well-being.

- **Inability to say no**: Without the ability to set clear boundaries, we may find ourselves struggling to refuse requests or demands from others, even when doing so would be in our best interest. This can result in a loss of control over our own lives and a sense of powerlessness. It is important to recognize the importance of establishing healthy boundaries in order to cultivate a deep sense of self-respect, regain authority in our own lives, and connect more fully with our own needs and desires.

Five steps to set boundaries:

1. **Identify** your boundaries: Start by identifying what your personal boundaries are. This means thinking about what is important to you, what you are and are not comfortable with, and what you need to feel safe and respected in your relationships and interactions with others.

2. **Communicate** your boundaries: Once you've identified your boundaries, communicate them clearly and assertively to others. This means being direct and specific about what you need and

expect from others, and not apologizing or minimizing your needs.

3. **Be consistent** It's important to be consistent in enforcing your boundaries. This means following through with consequences when someone violates your boundaries, and not allowing others to take advantage of you or push your limits.

4. **Practice self-care** Setting and enforcing boundaries can be diffi-cult, so it's important to prioritize self-care and self-compassion. Take time to rest, recharge, and practice self-care activities that help you feel grounded and centered.

5. **Evaluate and adjust** Boundaries are not set in stone and may need to be adjusted over time as circumstances change. Evaluate your boundaries periodically and make adjustments as necessary to ensure that they are still meeting your needs and helping you to feel safe and respected in your relationships and interactions with others.

By following these steps, you can set healthy boundaries that protect your well-being and help you feel empowered and confident in your relationships and interactions with others.

THE NEED FOR ACCEPTANCE

The yearning for acceptance is a fundamental and universal human desire. It is the desire to feel valued, loved, and validated by others. Unfortunately, this deep-seated need is often linked to the fear of judg-ment. We may worry that if we don't conform to certain social norms or expectations, others will reject or judge us negatively.

When we feel a strong need for acceptance, we may engage in be-haviors or attitudes that make us more likable or acceptable to others. This may include seeking approval or validation from others. While the need for acceptance is a natural and valid human desire, it can also be limiting if we allow it to dictate our behaviors or attitudes.

Excessive craving for acceptance can lead to a detrimental impact on our well-being and behavior. Therefore, it is important to note that having an unquenchable thirst to be accepted can result in adverse effects.

Some negative traits associated with this yearning include:

1. **People Pleasing:** When our need for acceptance becomes overwhelming, we may fall prey to people-pleasing, sacrificing our values and needs to satisfy those of others. This can result in a lack of healthy boundaries, diminished self-worth, and an inability to make choices in our best interest.

2. **Approval-seeking**: At times, we may be absorbed in pursuing external approval and validation to the point where we overlook the wisdom of our instincts and beliefs. This narrow focus can give rise to feelings of self-doubt and a heavy dependence on extrinsic validation.

3. **Conformity**: To be accepted by others, we may feel undue pressure to conform to social norms or expectations, even if they don't align with our values or beliefs. This can bring about a lack of authenticity and difficulty expressing our true selves.

4. **Fear of rejection:** The need for acceptance can also lead to a strong fear of rejection or criticism from others, which can cause us to avoid taking risks or pursuing our goals.

5. **Self-doubt**: When we rely too heavily on external validation, we may struggle with self-doubt and a lack of confidence in our own abilities and worth.

It's important to recognize when the need for acceptance is becoming excessive or harmful and to work on cultivating self-awareness, self-acceptance, and a healthy sense of self-worth. By doing so, we can learn to balance our need for acceptance with our own values and priorities and build a stronger sense of confidence and resilience.

Breaking the negativity of the need to be accepted can be challenging, but it is possible with self-awareness, practice, and patience. Here are some strategies that may help:

1. **Cultivate self-awareness:** Start by cultivating a heightened awareness of your thoughts, emotions, and actions regarding the human desire for acceptance. Take note of instances in which you may be seeking affirmation from external sources or conforming to societal norms, and ask yourself if these actions align with your values and priorities.

2. **Challenge negative beliefs:** Identify any detrimental thought patterns you may possess regarding your self-worth or acceptance. Engage in a dialogue with these assumptions by questioning their validity and evaluating how they impact your overall emotional and mental health.

3. **Practice self-acceptance:** Focus on cultivating a sense of self-acceptance and self-love, *regardless* of external validation. Practice self-compassion and give yourself grace and respect, even when you make mistakes or face rejection.

4. **Set boundaries:** Establishing firm boundaries around your time and energy is necessary for life. It's critical to honor your own needs, values, and priorities. When you do so, your inner spirit will soar, and you'll unlock new levels of happiness and fulfillment."

5. **Build a supportive community:** Surround yourself with people who support and validate your authentic self rather than those who pressure you to conform to their expectations. Seek out community and support systems that align with your values and priorities.

By breaking free from the negativity of seeking external validation, we embark on a transformational journey that requires patience, effort, and time. Admittedly, it is a challenging process, but practicing self-awareness, self-acceptance, and setting healthy boundaries could effectively catalyze the foundation of a more authentic sense of self-worth.

Setting healthy boundaries worksheet

1. Identify areas of your life where you need to set boundaries: Write down the areas of your life where you feel that your boundaries are being violated or where you need to set limits.

   ____

   ____

2. Define your boundaries: Define your boundaries clearly, so that you know what is acceptable and what is not. Write down your boundaries in a clear and concise manner.

   ____

   ____

3. **Communicate your boundaries:** Communicate your boundaries clearly and assertively to the people who need to know. Be firm but also respectful.

4. **Practice saying "no":** Learn to say "no" when your boundaries are being violated, or you are being asked to do something you don't want to do.

5. **Follow through:** Once you have set your boundaries, it is essential to follow through on them. Be consistent and stick to your limits, even if it is difficult.
   Reflect on your progress: Reflect on how setting boundaries has impacted your life. Write down any positive changes you have noticed and any challenges you have faced. ____

Remember, setting healthy boundaries is an ongoing process, so be patient with yourself and continue to work on it.

6

Chapter Six - Taking Action and Stepping Outside Your Comfort Zone

It is crucial to take action to step outside of one's comfort zone to break free from the fear of judgment. Remaining within a familiar, safe area can lead to stagnation and hinder growth and potential. Fear of judgment often causes us to shy away from taking risks or trying new things that may challenge us. However, such avoidance can prevent us from being exposed to new opportunities and learning new skills to help us achieve our goals. By stepping outside our comfort zone and confronting our fears, we can cultivate resilience and confidence in our ability to navigate challenges and uncertainty. We can also gain new perspectives and insights to facilitate personal growth and development.

Furthermore, when we challenge ourselves and take risks, we have the potential to ignite a spark that inspires others to do the same. By sharing our experiences and triumphs, we can help others break free from their fears and self-imposed limitations. Stepping outside our comfort zone can be daunting and anxiety-inducing, but it can also be enriching and empower us to reach new heights. It allows us to push beyond our self-doubts and limitations, instilling a renewed sense of resilience, confidence, and an openness to discovering unimagined possibilities for growth and achievement.

Identifying your goals and taking action to achieve them involves several steps:

1. **Reflect on your values:** Start by reflecting on your values and what are matters most to you. This can help you identify goals aligned with your core beliefs and priorities.

2. **Brainstorm potential goals:** List goals that align with your values and interests. Don't worry about feasibility or practicality at this stage; brainstorm as many ideas as possible.

3. **Prioritize your goals:** Review your list of potential goals and prioritize them based on their importance and feasibility. Consider which goals are most meaningful to you and which are achievable within your current resources and timeframe.

4. **Break down your goals into lesser steps:** Once you have identified them, break them down into smaller, achievable steps. This can help you avoid feeling overwhelmed and motivate you as you work towards your larger goals.

5. **Create an action plan:** Develop an action plan outlining your steps to achieve your goals. Set definite, measurable, and achievable goals for each step, and establish a timeline for completion.

Take action: Finally, take action to implement your action plan and work towards your goals. Stay focused on your priorities and adjust your plan to stay on track.

The path toward achieving your goals requires patience, diligent effort, and unwavering persistence. Maintain an energetic, unwavering motivation and unyielding focus, and do not allow setbacks or obstacles to demoralize you. With steadfast dedication comes hard work, at which point, attaining your goals and unlocking your full potential, a life of abundance and success awaits you.

Here are some strategies for stepping outside your comfort zone and facing your fears:

1. **Start small**: Start by taking small steps beyond the confines of your comfort zone, perhaps by savoring exotic cuisine or charting a new route to your place of work. Slowly, progressively, ascend towards more imposing challenges.

2. **Reframe your mindset:** Rather than fixating on the potential risks and adverse outcomes, shift your attention towards the possible benefits and positive results of confronting the very thing you fear. Liberating yourself from this fear can offer a whole new perspective on life, one that's full of opportunity and empowerment. Don't let apprehension control and inhibit you. Take that first bold step towards freedom and watch as your world transforms before your eyes."

1. **Visualize success:** Picture yourself winning and achieving your goal, imagining how you will feel and what you will gain from overcoming your fear.

2. **Seek support:** Surround yourself with a network of compassionate, benevolent, and encouraging individuals who bolster your morale, stimulate your growth, and fortify your willpower. Be receptive to the sagacious counsel and wisdom of those who have faced and vanquished similar misgivings, challenges, and tribulations.

3. **Practice relaxation techniques:** Learning relaxation techniques, such as the practice of deep breathing, the discipline of meditation, or the art of yoga, can profoundly mitigate the intensity of your anxiety and soothe your nerves.

4. **Take action despite fear:** Take action even if you are not entirely ready or confident, and have the courage to face your fears. The more you practice getting out of your comfort zone, the more comfortable and confident you will become. Trust your inner self.

5. **Celebrate successes**: Take time to honor and appreciate your victories, no matter how seemingly insignificant they may be. Acknowledge the strides and achievements you've made along your journey.

Stepping beyond the confines of what's familiar and comfortable is no easy feat but vital for personal expansion and development. With diligent practice and determined perseverance, you can leap beyond those fears and establish a path toward realizing your dreams.

7

Chapter Seven - Celebrating Your Success and Embracing Your Uniqueness

Celebrating and embracing your unique self is pivotal because doing so helps build and cultivate self-esteem, confidence, and a favorable self-image. When you recognize and commemorate your strengths and accomplishments, you reinforce a sense of self-worth and acknowledge your own value.

Furthermore, embracing your distinctive qualities allows you to recognize and appreciate the diversity in others. Instead of feeling insecure or threatened by differences among others, you can celebrate and learn from them. This creates a more optimistic and all-encompassing environment for yourself and those around you.

You open yourself to a more enriching and fulfilling existence by embracing your individuality and honoring your unique qualities. Through this, you may uncover undiscovered talents and unlock new abilities or use your exceptional viewpoint and experiences to catalyze positive change in your community. Ultimately, learning to celebrate and accept your true self empowers you to live authentically and confidently, paving the way for a happier and more satisfying life.

Learning to celebrate your accomplishments and appreciate your unique strengths and qualities takes practice, but here are some tips to get started:

1. **Keep a journal:** Write down your accomplishments, big and small, and reflect on the strengths and qualities that helped you achieve them.

2. **Surround yourself with positive influences:** Share time with those who will celebrate your accomplishments and appreciate your unique qualities. Avoid persons who bring you down or make you feel insecure.

3. **Practice self-care:** Take care of yourself physically, emotionally, and mentally. Take part in activities that make you feel good about yourself, such as exercise, meditation, or creative hobbies.

4. **Reframe your mindset:** Instead of focusing on your shortcomings, consciously focus on your strengths and unique qualities. Remind yourself of the positive impact you have on the world.

5. **Set achievable goals:** Set practical goals for yourself and celebrate your progress. Each time you reach a goal, acknowledge your hard work and accomplishments.

6. **Embrace failure as a learning opportunity:** Don't be afraid to fail. Instead, view failures as opportunities to learn and grow. Take the lessons you've learned and apply them to future endeavors.

7. **Practice gratitude:** Take time daily to express gratitude for what you appreciate about yourself and your life. This can help transfer your focus to the positive aspects of your life and boost your sense of self-worth.

Remember, celebrating your accomplishments and appreciating your unique strengths and qualities takes time and practice. But by focusing on the positive and surrounding yourself with supportive influences, you can build a stronger sense of self-worth and lead a more fulfilling life.

Cultivating gratitude and positivity is a potent and transcendent way to fuel your confidence and transcend the fear of judgment that often binds us. Here are some highly effective strategies to help you cultivate and harness gratitude and positivity:

1. **Practice mindfulness:** Every day, make a conscious effort to fully engage in the moment and reflect on the blessings that abound in your life. This can be as effortless as taking a few deep breaths and mindfully observing the splendor surrounding you.

2. **Keep a gratitude journal:** Write down three things you are grateful for each day. This can be a simple activity, but it can tremendously influence your mindset.

3. **Surround yourself with positivity:** Surround yourself with individuals who radiate positivity, upliftment, and unwavering support, for they are the ones who will elevate and transform you. Strive to steer clear of individuals who drag you down or evoke feelings of insecurity, for their toxicity will hinder your journey toward self-discovery and growth.

4. **Focus on solutions, not problems:** When encountering a difficulty, focus on discovering solutions rather than fixating on the issue. This approach can empower you and strengthen your confidence in surmounting barriers.

5. **Practice self-care:** Engage in the sacred art of self-care, nurturing your physical, emotional, and mental well-being with practices that evoke joy, peace, and vitality. Whether moving your body through invigorating exercise, stilling your mind in meditation, or expressing your soul through creative pursuits, prioritize the activities that nourish and uplift you. By honorably tending to yourself, you radiate the gifts of abundant life to those around you.

6. **Give back:** By offering a helping hand to others, we can intentionally nourish gratitude and positivity within ourselves. Consider volunteering at a local non-profit, contributing to a charitable organization, or extending a gracious gesture to a needy friend.

7. **Celebrate your accomplishments:** Take time to recognize and celebrate your wins, no matter how minor. This can help boost your confidence and reinforce your sense of self-worth. THROW YOUR OWN PARTY!

One essential aspect of self-celebration is to refrain from depending on others to validate your existence. Years back, when I hit the grand milestone of turning sixty, I took up the responsibility of celebrating the woman I had become and the one I aim to evolve into. Driven by passion and excitement, I organized an exquisite party at a grand mansion fully in my control. From dedicated servers to a professional photographer, I left no stone unturned to make my celebration extraordinary. White was the theme, and diamonds and pearls became the decor inspiration. With the DJ's sound engulfing the hall, I danced and danced, reveling in my party's grandeur, all honoring myself, my uniqueness, and my journey. My loved ones were my witnesses, and witnessing me shine in such grandiosity stimulated their admiration and respect for the woman I have become.

By cultivating gratitude and positivity, one can shift their mindset from fear and self-doubt to confidence and empowerment. There was a season in my life when I would have thought it was absurd or inappropriate to celebrate my existence in such a way. Still, I quickly realized that for all the trials and tribulations I had endured and overcome, I must celebrate who I am. By celebrating myself, I am also celebrating my Creator. When one takes the time to be grateful for all the blessings in their life, they can overcome the fear of judgment and fully embrace their unique strengths and qualities with grace and elegance.

8

Chapter Eight - Moving Forward with Unstoppable Confidence

Moving Forward with Unstoppable Confidence is like erecting a force field around your life. It entails the understanding that life's gusts may indeed blow but that they should not determine who you are or who you are becoming. You must, without hesitation, believe in yourself, your talents, and aspirations. Keep in mind that no one but you have the power to impede your progress. You are powerful, dynamic, and unconstrained; create your desired life.

Here are some insightful journal prompts that can assist you on your journey towards continued growth and confident self-discovery

1. What are my top strengths and how can I use them to achieve my goals?

2. What are my areas of growth and how can I work on them to become a better version of myself?

3. What are some limiting beliefs that I need to let go of in order to grow and build my confidence?

4. What are some new skills or knowledge I want to acquire to enhance my personal and professional development?

5. What are some small steps I can take every day to build my confidence and overcome my fears?

6. How can I surround myself with people who uplift and inspire me to reach my full potential?

7. What are some self-care practices that can help me maintain a positive and resilient mindset?

8. What are some accomplishments that I am proud of, and how can I use them to build my confidence?

9. What are some fears that are holding me back, and how can I face them head-on to grow and build my confidence?

10. What are some affirmations or positive self-talk that I can repeat to myself daily to build my confidence and self-esteem?

____

Remember, constructing solid self-confidence and self-esteem is not an overnight task but a continuous, ongoing journey that requires unwavering dedication and persistent introspection. You can create a blueprint for everlasting transformation and progression through journaling and self-reflection.

AFFIRMATIONS

Affirmations are positive statements that a person can use to challenge and replace negative self-talk. They are essential in breaking free from the fear of judgment because they help to reframe negative beliefs and thoughts into positive ones. In addition, affirmations can cultivate self-love, confidence, and a sense of self-acceptance.

When a person repeats affirmations regularly, they begin to internalize them and believe them on a deeper level. This can help to shift their perspective and create a more positive self-image. Affirmations can also serve as a reminder of a person's values, goals, and strengths, which can be especially helpful during times of self-doubt or fear of judgment.

Below are some affirmations to help you maintain your progress and remain motivated when faced with new challenges:

Affirmations:

1. I am resilient and capable of overcoming all challenge that comes my way.
2. I am strong and determined to reach my highest potential.
3. I am able to achieve my goals and dreams.
4. I am worthy of success and happiness, and every day in every way, I am making it happen.
5. I am grateful for my progress and excited for what's to come.
6. I am confident in my ability to navigate any obstacle.
7. I am deserving of love, respect, and success.
8. I am limitless and able to achieve my greatest desires.
9. I am unstoppable, worthy, powerful, and strong.
10. I am free to be unapologetically me.

9

Conclusion - Embracing Fear of Judgment and Finding Freedom

Fear is a natural human emotion that responds to a perceived threat or danger. It is a vital and powerful mechanism to keep you safe, yet it can also be overwhelming and debilitating if it becomes too intense. Therefore, recognizing the presence of an unhealthy fear, which can cause you to freeze and become mentally paralyzed, is imperative. Without acknowledging and confronting this debilitating emotion, you'll be unable to move forward and create the fulfilling existence you deserve.

So many people have allowed the fear of judgment to rule their existence. They have become accustomed to living within the confines of a box, too afraid to express themselves fully. Yet, their inner being cries out for freedom, the liberty to move through life in their own unique way, at their own pace, and on their own schedule.

It's time to acknowledge that you, too, have been plagued with this debilitating challenge that had power over you. Acknowledge the events and characters in your life's story who played a significant role in living under the radar or playing it safe. We acknowledge because it did happen, it's a part of your life's history, but it doesn't have to play a starring role in your future. Now is the time to awaken to the endless possibilities that await you with open arms. Let yourself be guided by the Divine into the life of your deepest, most authentic desires.

Acknowledging the fear of judgment entails recognizing and embracing that one harbors a fear of being evaluated by others. This involves accepting the various emotions and physical sensations that arise when one feels the weight of judgment and comprehending the potential influence this fear can have on one's thoughts, actions, and overall well-being.

Acknowledging your fear of judgment is a crucial *first-step* in addressing it. This practice enables you to be more self-aware and mindful of your thoughts and actions, allowing you to recognize the triggers contributing to your fear. Additionally, it promotes increased self-compassion and understanding as you acknowledge that fear of judgment is a common yet normal experience many people struggle with daily.

When you recognize and honor your fear of judgment, you open the door to exploring and challenging the negative thoughts and beliefs that underlie it. You cultivate kindness and care towards yourself and reach out to others who can offer guidance and support. By acknowledging your fear of judgment, you take an empowering step towards managing it with greater ease and grace and opening yourself to a more vibrant and fulfilling life.

Acknowledging is not about placing blame but instead gaining awareness of your circumstances. Doing so allows you to take control of your life and move forward as the driver of your own story. No longer a passenger, you hold the keys to your destiny.

Embracing the fear of judgment involves acknowledging and accepting its existence without allowing it to control or limit your actions and decisions. It requires recognizing that feeling anxious or afraid in certain situations is normal. *Taking-Steps* to overcome it means facing your fears, challenging negative thoughts and beliefs, practicing self-compassion and self-care, and seeking support from others.

It also entails taking small steps toward your goals and gradually building your confidence and resilience. Although it may not happen overnight, daily practice will lead to the day when you no longer struggle to be unapologetically yourself.

Embracing the fear of judgment is an empowering experience, allowing you to control your thoughts and actions rather than letting your fears dictate your life. As a result, you will develop greater self-awareness of what you genuinely love and care about and gain the courage to try new things that your former self would have shunned out of fear of judgment. Embracing the fear of judgment can be challenging but also a transformative and rewarding experience. By facing your fears head-on and ***taking-steps*** towards overcoming them, you can build greater confidence, resilience, and self-acceptance, ultimately leading to a more fulfilling and authentic life.

Do you yearn for true personal freedom? The kind that comes with knowing yourself profoundly and blossoming into the fullest expression of who you indeed are? If so, the ***first step*** is to shed the yokes of judgment and self-sabotage that hold you back. Rise up, cast aside the chains of others' opinions, and free yourself to laugh, create, and simply be. The path to true freedom lies within, waiting for you to claim it.

A marvelous world of self-assurance and self-respect reveals itself when one is released from the bondage of self-judgment. One can boldly display their true essence, pursue their passions and interests unhindered, and venture into the unknown with courage and confidence. Just picture one's self reveling in the pure joy of following your favorite activity, all while experiencing complete inner tranquility and harmony with your higher self. Long gone are the days of being held captive in the Valley of self-doubt or living in the constant dread of receiving judgmental blows. True freedom is to be set free in one's mind, heart, and spirit. It was created by love, thrives on love, exists, moves, and has its being in love. True freedom is no longer anticipating impending punishment but believing that one was meant to live life to the fullest potential, unrestrained by limitations, to blaze new trails, to dream big dreams, and to become all they were created to be. To believe in oneself and the divine master of the universe who designed one's life to shine brilliantly, imbued with boldness and uniqueness – being unapologetically one's true self!